The Castle Book

by Michael Berenstain

David McKay Co., Inc.
New York

Blarney Castle

Balmoral

Elsinore~ Castle of Prince Hamlet

Carnarvon

The Tower of London

Ghent

The "Mouse" Castle~ Tdl Station on the Rhine

Chateau Gaillard

The Bastille of Paris

Wildenstein Castle

Chateau Poitiers

Segovia~ Castle of Isabella

The Castle of Chillon

The Tower of Constance

Manzanares

Castel St. Angelo, Fortress of the Popes

Library of Congress Cataloging in Publication Data
Berenstain, Michael.
The castle book.
SUMMARY: Briefly describes the purpose and construction of
European castles built during the Middle Ages.
1. Castles—Juvenile literature. [1. Castles]
I. Title.
NA7710.B47   940.1   77-263
ISBN 0-679-20403-2

10 9 8 7 6 5 4 3 2 1
Manufactured in the United States of America

Great Castles of the World

Kalmar
Castle

Heilsberg~
Castle of the
Teutonic Knights

Karlstein Castle, Prague

Kiev~
The Wooden Castle
of Prince Vladimir

The Kremlin, Mos
Castle of Ivan the Gre

Forchtenstein Castle,
Austria

The "Black Tower"
of the Sultans

Smederevo~ Castle
on the Danube

The "Krak" of th
Knights Hospita

The Acropolis,
Athens~
Ancient Temple
used as Castle

The Castle of Kyrenia,
Cyprus

Long ago, kings and queens lived in great fortresses called castles. High walls and strong towers kept the rulers and their courts safe from their enemies.

The first European castles were built over one thousand years ago. They were made of wood and earth and had high hilltop towers surrounded by walls and ditches. Inside the walls were stables and storerooms.

Although these castles were strongly built, they were easy to set on fire. This is why rulers began building castles of stone.

Some early stone castles were tall and square
and topped by small watchtowers.

Others were wide and round with central courtyards.

One of the earliest and largest stone castles, the Tower of London, is still used today to store the crown jewels and old arms and armor.

But the nobles of long ago decided to build larger and stronger castles.

Here is an example of the kind of castle they built. It was so large that it was like a small city. Hundreds of people lived and worked inside its walls.

catapult

watchtower

gatehouse

drawbridge

stables

gate

inner wall

outer wall

moat

courtyard

the keep

watchtower

royal chamber

chapel

great hall

guardroom

kitchen

dungeon

escape tunnel

The entrance to this castle was well guarded. A visitor had to cross the drawbridge over the moat and pass through the main gate.

Above the entrance was a room where a guard raised and lowered the drawbridge and gate.

On top of the gatehouse was a catapult—a weapon that was used to shoot large rocks at enemy armies.

Beyond the gatehouse was a wide courtyard, where the everyday work of the castle was done. There the blacksmith shod horses, peasants tended livestock, and the boys of the castle trained to be knights.

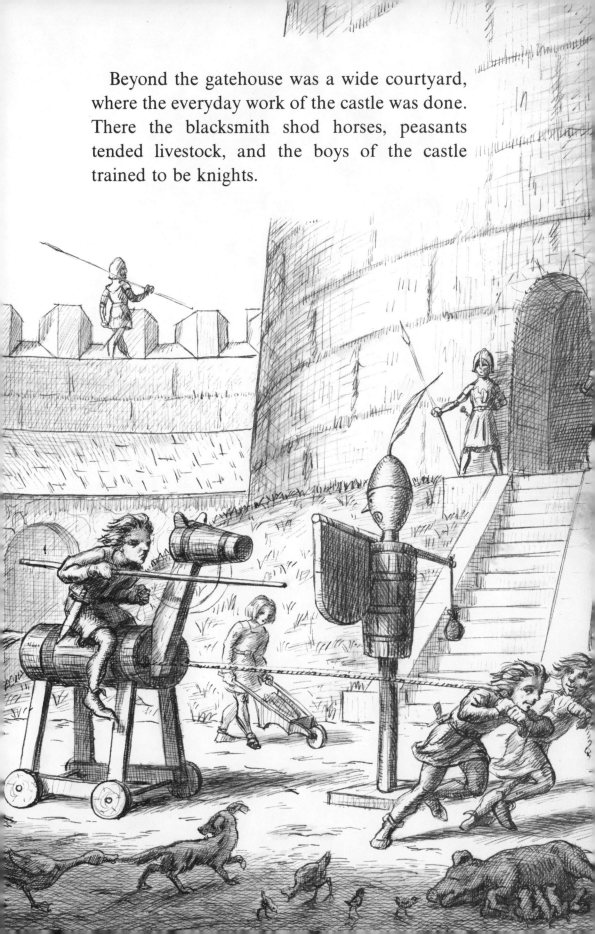

Beyond the courtyard was the inner wall. And behind the wall were the chapel and the great tower, called the keep.

The chapel was like a little church. Everyone in the castle went there to worship.

The keep itself had many floors. Deep under-ground was the dungeon, where the ruler's prisoners were kept.

On the floors above the dungeon were the kitchen, where food for feasts was prepared,

the guardroom, where the castle's knights lived,

and the royal chamber, where the ladies of the castle often worked, sewing and weaving tapestries.

Banquets were held in the keep's great hall. During the feasts, the guests were entertained by musicians, jugglers, and dancing bears.

At the top of the keep was the watchtower. From there, soldiers could look out and see the rest of the castle and the countryside beyond it.

This is what most castles were like. But there were other kinds as well.

Some castles guarded seacoasts.

Some blocked desert roads.

Other castles overlooked mountain passes or protected great cities.

Many castles were built in places that were easy to defend.

The Castle of Chillon in Switzerland stood on an island in a lake.

The Troyenstein castle in Germany
was built on top of a steep cliff.

If castles were not strongly built,
they were quickly captured by
enemy armies.

One of the ways an army attacked a castle was to push huge towers up against the castle's walls. Then a drawbridge was lowered, and soldiers poured across it and into the castle.

Most castles could be defended against this
kind of attack. But there was one weapon that
very few castles could withstand—the cannon.
Since cannon fire could knock down the thick-
est walls, the invention of the cannon brought
about the end of the age of castles.

Today, most castles are in ruins, destroyed by years of war and neglect.

But, in a way, the age of castles is not over.
Only when it is forgotten will it truly end.

728.8 Berenstain, Michael
B
2371   The castle book

IIIENDE   CCHOOL

728.8 Berenstain, Michael   2371
B
         The castle book

WENDELL L CROSS SCHOOL

DATE	BORROWER'S NAME	
MAY 3 0 1979	Darre D Z	
APR 25 198	herr D	
MAY 2 1980		27

© THE BAKER & TAYLOR CO.